Dedicated to all the spirited toddlers embarking on the adventure of words and speech. With a special shout out to my gorgeous daughter, Ehinome, whose relatable style of expressing those initial words has been the inspiration behind this book.

Copyright @2024 by Webilor Ediale
All rights reserved. No part of this book may be reproduced or used in any manner without written permission of the copyright owner, except for the use of quotations in a book review.
ISBN-13: 978-17395324-3-7
For more information, or to book an event, visit our website at
www.webilorediale.com

I WANT MASKIT!

WEBILOR EDIALE

TRULY SANDRA

THIS BOOK BELONGS TO

there lived a very happy and vibrant 2-year-old toddler named Nome.

Nome resided with her loving mother, Webi, her caring father, Steve, and her energetic 5-year-old brother, Sele.

One day, as the sun bathed the kitchen in a golden glow,

CHOP CHOP

Nome, with her cute little feet, shuffled into the room where her mum was busy cooking.

Looking down at her precious daughter,
Webi smiled and asked,

"HI NOME, ARE YOU OKAY?"

Nome, in response, looked up at her mum and sweetly rubbed her tiny tummy with a little smile.

"ARE YOU HUNGRY, MY LOVELY BABY GIRL?" her mum asked.

Nome, with a vigorous nod of her head, confirmed her hunger.

"Okay now, let's get you something to nibble on while mum finishes off lunch.

WHAT WOULD YOU LIKE?"

Tugging at her mum's skirt again,

Nome pointed at one of the kitchen cabinets.

"Okay," said her mum, "let's see what we have here."

Opening the cabinet, she suggested,

"Do you want the plantain chips?"
Nome responded with a spirited, "Nh, nh!"
shaking her head in disapproval.

"How about some dried fruits then?" asked Webi. Again, Nome shook her head with disapproval.

"Perhaps you'll like some crisps?" her mum offered, only for Nome to express her distaste by looking away and pushing her hands forward.

"Nh, nh!"

"So WHAT DO YOU WANT, NOME?" asked her mum.

With a big smile on her face, Nome shouted, "MASK IT!" and pointed at the same cabinet.

A bit confused, Webi asked, "What's Maskit?"
Nome eagerly repeated, "Maskit."

Not understanding, Webi lifted Nome into her arms. Nome pointed again at the kitchen cabinet, repeating, "Maskit."

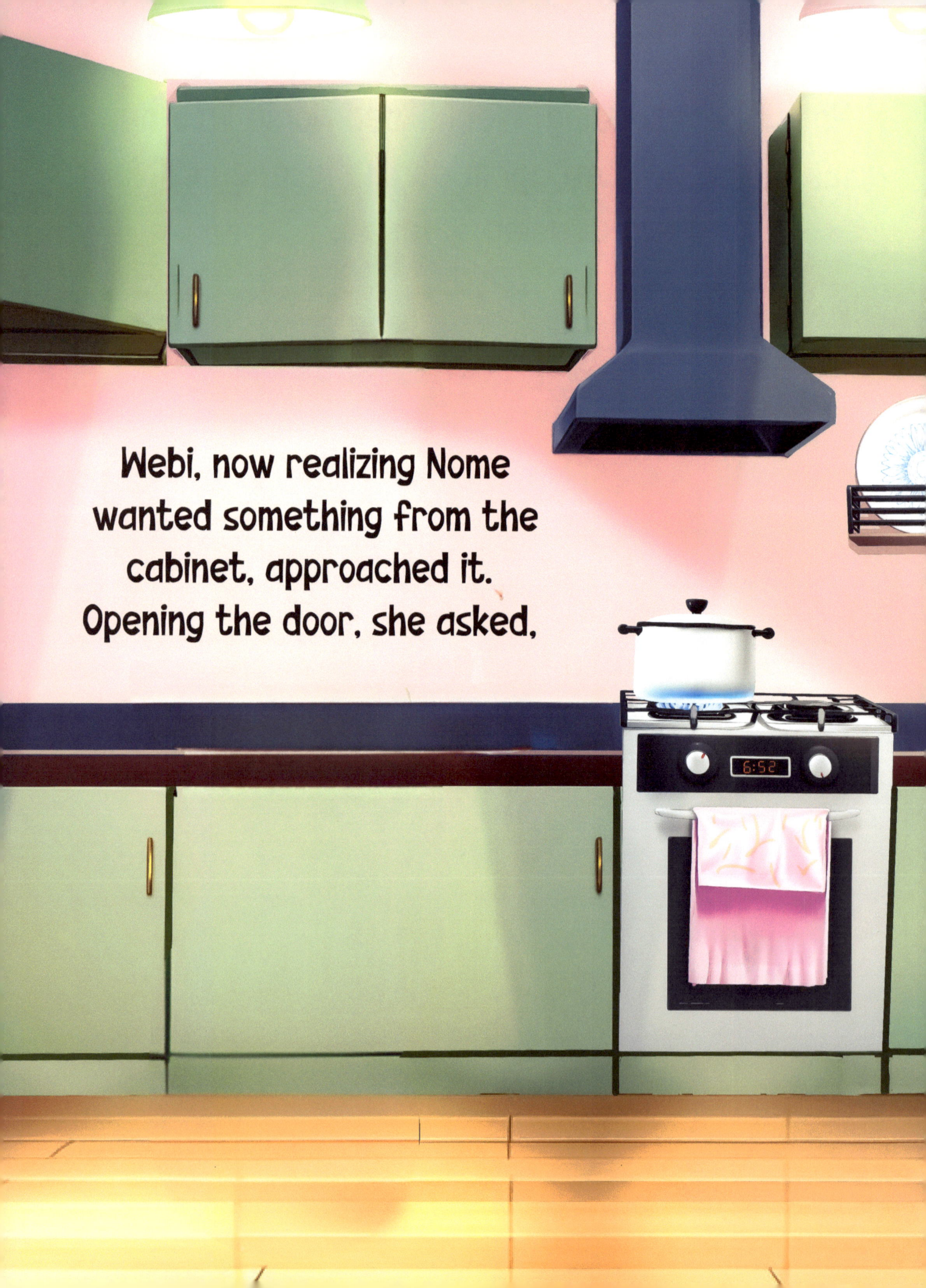

Webi, now realizing Nome wanted something from the cabinet, approached it. Opening the door, she asked,

Nome's cute head peeped into the cabinet; with smiling and shiny, bright eyes,

she grabbed a pack of biscuits. Turning around with a loud voice, she proudly screamed at her mum,

MASKIT!

Webi chuckled, "Oh, Nome, you mean BISCUIT?" But Nome, in disagreement, said, "Nh, Nh, MASKIT."

"Okay," said Webi as she put Nome down and opened the pack of biscuits.

Nome sat on her high chair, gladly enjoying her biscuits, while mum finished her cooking.

Webi then called out to her husband and son, "STEVE, SELE, lunch is ready!"

As she walked towards Nome, her tummy made a loud rumbling noise.

"Goodness me, Nome, you must be hungry?" Webi exclaimed.

"Maskit!" called out Nome. "**NO NOME**, no more biscuit, it's time to have a proper meal."

And so, all the family joyfully gathered at the table and had a delicious lunch together.

WERE YOU ABLE TO IDENTIFY ALL 30 SIGHT WORDS IN THIS BOOK?
JOIN NOME TO READ THEM OUT LOUD!

THE	AT
AND	BE
OF	HAVE
A	FROM
TO	ONE
IN	BY
IS	NOT
YOU	WHAT
IT	ALL
FOR	WE
ON	SAID
ARE	BUT
AS	DO
WITH	SHE
SO	NO

Don't forget to get the accompanying Activity Workbook of I Want Maskit for more fun activities.

ACCOMPANYING ACTIVITY WORKBOOK

AWARD WINNING BOOK SERIES

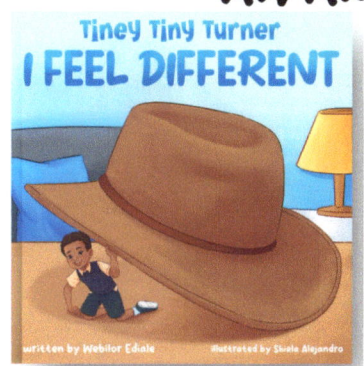  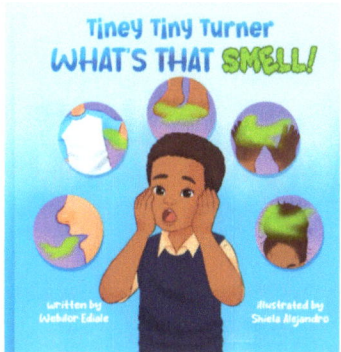 

OTHER BOOKS FROM WEBILOR EDIALE

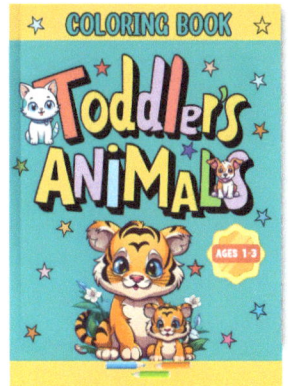   

For more information, please visit www.webilorediale.com

If you enjoyed this book consider leaving us a review on this link: https://mybook.to/IWantMaskit or by scanning the QR code to help support and enable us bring more books your way.

www.ingramcontent.com/pod-product-compliance
Lightning Source LLC
Chambersburg PA
CBHW041537040426
42446CB00002B/134